...as in Service in the Old 2th ——
...t of the Year 1780 when he was
...Sappers & Miners & is still in

...ted ———— D. Bushnell Capt. & Senior
Officer in the Corps of
Sappers & Miners.

...out in the Old 2th Regt
...he served part of the

...ming Suit.

BUSHNELL'S
SUBMARINE

BUSHNELL'S SUBMARINE

The Best Kept Secret of the American Revolution

ARTHUR S. LEFKOWITZ

SCHOLASTIC NONFICTION

An imprint of

SCHOLASTIC

Library of Congress Cataloging-in-Publication Data

Lefkowitz, Arthur S.

Bushnell's submarine: the best kept secret of the American Revolution / by Arthur Lefkowitz.

p. cm.

ISBN 0-439-74352-4

1. Submarines (Ships)—United States—History—18th century. 2. Submarine warfare—United States—History—18th century. 3. Bushnell, David, b. 1740. 4. United States—History—Revolution, 1775–1783—Naval operations. I. Title.

V858.L43 2006

973.3'5—dc22

2005042645

10 9 8 7 6 5 4 3 2 1   06 07 08 09 10

Printed in the U.S.A.

First printing, March 2006

Art Direction: Tatiana Sperhacke

Book Design: Kay Petronio

To my children, Amy and Joshua,
who always like a good story

Contents

CHAPTER ONE

New York at War

AT FIRST GLANCE, New York harbor seemed like a peaceful place on the night of September 6, 1776. It was a cloudy night with a fresh breeze and rain at times. However, a closer look at the harbor revealed the outlines of hundreds of ships, whose presence was confirmed by lanterns hanging from their decks and rigging. Beyond them, flickering lights were visible on nearby Staten Island and western Long Island (modern Brooklyn). They were coming from the campfires of the large British army that surrounded the city. In the opposite direction, lights were also visible from New York City, located on the southern tip of Manhattan Island. They were from the forts and barricades occupied by the Continental

(American) army, defending the city and civilians who had not fled the war zone. Everyone in the metropolis appeared to be sleeping, but a careful observer could see Continental artillerymen manning the cannons that defended the city and squads of soldiers patrolling its blockaded streets and waterfront.

There was also activity on the dock at the bottom of Whitehall Street, where a group of American officers had gathered in the darkness. The men on the dock were watching an unusual sight: a strange-looking craft, bobbing just barely above the surface of the water, that was attached by ropes to two big rowboats called whaleboats. Even in the darkness, one could see that the top of the strange machine was made of brass, with glass portholes on all sides and two brass tubes pointing straight up into the sky. The officers on the dock spoke in excited whispers as they watched the whaleboat crews begin to tow the machine out into the harbor, their oars wrapped in rags to muffle the sound. The Americans gathered on the dock were among the few men who knew that the strange craft under tow was an "underwater machine": a submarine called the *American Turtle*, which was setting out to sink one of the big Royal Navy warships anchored in the harbor.

CHAPTER TWO

Introducing David Bushnell

THE MAN RESPONSIBLE for the *American Turtle* was also on the dock that night. His name was David Bushnell, and he is an example of a fascinating breed of Americans called "Yankee tinkerers." They were dreamers and inventors who created amazing machines, often working alone in sheds and barns with simple tools and little formal education. Bushnell was different from some of the other homespun inventors: Despite being born on a small farm in Connecticut, he had attended Yale College (today's Yale University) in New Haven, Connecticut, where he studied science and mathematics. He was born in 1740 and entered Yale in 1771, making him thirty-one years old when he started college. It was beyond the usual age for a man to go to college (women did not go to college at the time), and Bushnell was called "the old man" by his classmates. He had desperately wanted to get a college education earlier in his life, but his father was a poor farmer, and it took David years to scrape together the money to pay for school. He raised some of the money by working in a Connecticut shipyard that was located near his boyhood home in Old Saybrook, Connecticut. This work experience gave him some pence (coins) and an introduction to the principles of ship construction. Even after he had the money for school, David studied with the Reverend John Devotion, a local clergyman and scholar, who tutored him in subjects including natural philosophy (science) and Latin, while a fellow townsman, named Elias Tully, let David live in his house as a guest.

David Bushnell attended Yale for four years and graduated in the class of 1775. During the same period, America was moving toward war with Britain over the growing fear that the British government was trying to control the lives of the colonists (the decision to declare independence from Britain came later in the war). The Boston Tea Party (December 1773), for example, happened while David was at Yale. With war approaching, many of his fellow students formed a militia company and prepared to defend their liberties. David, who shared their patriotism, turned his scientific mind to figuring out how to sink the Royal Navy. He selected an important way to aid the patriot cause because Britain had the largest and best navy in the world. The Royal Navy could easily plunder American merchant ships at sea, ravage the coast, and burn towns, while the colonists had few warships and little means to quickly build and arm them. Bushnell was determined to find a way to destroy enemy ships, and he turned to books for ideas. Thus, while his fellow students were drilling with muskets on New Haven's village green, Bushnell was in the Yale library reading about ancient schemes of sinking ships with "Greek fire" (flaming oil) or exploding "infernals" (mines).

CHAPTER THREE

Preparations for War

ON THE EVE of the American Revolution, the library at Yale contained about four thousand books. This is modest by today's standards, as it was about the size of a modern elementary school library. But books were expensive and difficult to obtain at the time, and Yale had one of the largest and most important libraries in colonial America. About a third of Yale's books survived the Revolutionary War and are among the prized possessions of the university.

Some of the surviving books include ideas and fanciful drawings of unusual ways to sink ships, and Bushnell is known to have referred to these books while he was a student. Among the ideas that he learned by reading was that a single underwater shot into the body (hull) of a ship was more deadly than a broadside of cannon fire directed at its deck and rigging. He learned how inventors had toyed with infernals—underwater cannons, rams, shooting torpedoes, and mines designed to sink ships.

The most promising type of infernal was called a mine. It was a device filled with gunpowder, designed to explode under the unprotected bottom of a warship. However, there were several technical problems to solve before building such a weapon, the most challenging being that gunpowder would not explode if it was wet, and there was no evidence at the time that gunpowder would create an explosion if it was detonated underwater. In addition, a flame or spark (a fuse) was necessary to make the powder explode.

Bushnell solved part of the problem by packing gunpowder into a waterproof wooden keg. He probably got the idea of how to ignite the powder by reading about the infernal, also called a "clock-machine," suggested by the Marquess of Worcester (an English naval officer) in 1655. The marquess speculated that a device containing gunpowder could be attached to the hull of a ship and triggered by a clock. Building on this idea, Bushnell designed a sturdy clock mechanism with an arm that snapped the trigger of a modified flintlock gun at a preset time. When the gun lock fired, a spark was created that detonated the powder. His idea looked promising, and Nehemiah Strong, Yale's patriotic professor of mathematics and natural philosophy, encouraged him to develop it.

With Professor Strong's support, Bushnell successfully exploded small infernals in secret tests. His experiments proved that an underwater explosion would not ripple harmlessly through the water but would create a concentrated, powerful blast. However, a much bigger explosion was necessary to blow a hole large enough to sink a ship. He knew he could build such a large device, but how would he deliver and attach it to the bottom of a ship without being seen? The answer was a submarine, and, with war approaching, Bushnell started to read everything in the Yale library on the subject.

He learned that the English were particularly fascinated with underwater travel and that they had been studying the concept for centuries. He found a great concept in a book titled *Inventions or Devices* that was published in 1578, during the reign of Queen Elizabeth I. The author was William Bourne, a gunner in Elizabeth's navy, whose idea was to build a craft with collapsible leather tanks, attached to its hull, into which water could enter through holes and be forced out with hand-turned screws. Bourne used the weight of the water to make his boat heavier and sink underwater. When water, lead, bricks, or any other material is used as a weight, it is called ballast, and Bourne's boat would sink when ballast (water) was poured into the leather tanks and return to the surface when the ballast was pushed back into the sea. His idea is the basic principle on which all modern submarines operate. Bourne never built a submarine, but his breakthrough concept of using water as ballast was employed by Bushnell two hundred years later.

Besides books, we know that the Yale library subscribed to magazines, published in England, that specialized in "Pieces of Wit, Humour or Intelligence, daily offer'd to the Publick," including scientific news and information. The most popular of these periodicals was *The Gentleman's Magazine*, which began publication in 1731 and continued well into the twentieth century. This publication included stories about underwater warfare, and we are certain, from the design of Bushnell's craft, that he read the submarine articles that appeared from time to time in *The Gentleman's*

The Fate of American College Libraries in the Revolutionary War

———— ◎ ————

THERE WERE EIGHT COLLEGES in America at the start of the American Revolution, including Harvard, Yale, and the College of William and Mary, and the academic center of each was its valuable library of books, magazines, and scientific instruments.

David Bushnell attended Yale, located in the seacoast town of New Haven, Connecticut. Fearing an attack by the British, Yale's library was moved inland to safety at the start of the war. Harvard did the same. However, the libraries at Princeton and King's College (now Columbia University) were not so lucky. An eyewitness reported that upon General Howe's entry into New York City, in September 1776, his soldiers plundered the King's College library. According to one account, "This was done with impunity, and the books publicly hawked about the town for sale by private soldiers, their trulls, and doxeys. I saw an Annual Register neatly bound and lettered, sold for a dram [a drink of whiskey, taken in one gulp]. . . . I saw in a public house upon Long Island nearly 40 books . . . under pawn from one dram to three drams each."

We are fortunate that Yale's library survived the war and that we can see the same scientific books and magazines that David Bushnell studied to get his ideas for building his submarine.

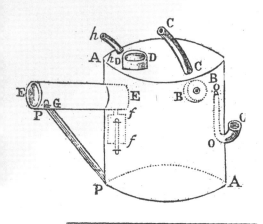

DIAGRAM OF A SUBMARINE FROM
THE 1747 *GENTLEMAN'S MAGAZINE*
This illustration was based on a
sketch by Denis Papin. It appeared
in a magazine article about how to
build a submarine that David
Bushnell is believed to have read
when he was a student at Yale.

Magazine. For example, the December 1747 issue included a story and drawings of a submarine designed by Denis Papin. His ideas included a waterproof hatch on top for a man to enter the sub and holes on the bottom of the craft for admitting and discharging water (ballast). Papin's craft also had tubes extending to the surface (snorkels) that allowed air to enter his submarine when it was submerged. Papin built two experimental vessels to test his ideas but never perfected a working submarine.

The Gentleman's Magazine also included stories about the work of another early inventor, Cornelius Jacobszoon Drebbel, who was probably the first man in history to travel underwater. He was a Dutch glassmaker and scientist working for the English. His idea was to slant the bow (front) of a covered boat with weights so that it would dive underwater when power was applied. Sailors seated on benches with oars inside the leather-covered boat provided the power. The oars extended through leather seals along the vessel's sides, with air pipes sticking out above the surface to provide a constant supply of oxygen for the large crew. Apparently, there was little forward motion, and the boat returned to the surface when the sailors stopped rowing. There is evidence that Drebbel built a boat that dived underwater and he demonstrated it in the Thames River, in London in 1620, with twelve men frantically pulling at the oars. Bushnell read about Drebbel's experiments, which, although impractical, gave him ideas about using waterproof seals, weights, and oars when he designed his submarine.

Bourne, Papin, and Drebbel made important contributions, but none of them built a submarine. To explain, there are four challenges to building a practical, working submarine: (1) how to keep it watertight and intact from outside water pressure; (2) how to maneuver it underwater; (3) how to provide an air supply when it is submerged; and (4) how to determine depth, location, and direction underwater. The inventors and scientists who preceded Bushnell solved pieces of the puzzle, but

Cornelius Jacobszoon Drebbel
(1572–1634)

———— ◎ ————

CORNELIUS DREBBEL was a Dutch inventor whose ideas were so unusual that he had the reputation of being a sorcerer. He was welcomed in 1604 by King James I to England, where he did much of his important work, including building a submersible "little ship" described as a "leather encased rowing boat." It was designed to carry twelve oarsmen and several passengers below the surface. According to one eyewitness account, "Drebbel and his crew, calmly dove down under the water [of the Thames River] and thus held the king, his court, and several thousand Londoners in excited expectation.... He called upon the several persons who had undergone the experiment with him to bear witness that they had had no discomfort under the river and when they chose risen to whatever height they liked."

He is believed to have used air tubes, supported on the surface by floats, to bring a continuous supply of oxygen into his craft. There are no known creditable descriptions or illustrations of Drebbel's submersible.

he was the first to bring all their ideas together, adding several of his own and applying them all in a practical manner to create the world's first submarine.

War broke out between the colonists and Britain on April 19, 1775, in Massachusetts, as Bushnell was completing his college education and working on the design of his submarine. A few days later (April 21), the news that the war had started reached New Haven, where it created great excitement and emotion on the Yale campus. With America at war and the college in turmoil, classes were suspended and the students were told to go home for an extended spring break. The school reopened on May 30, 1775, and Bushnell was among the returning seniors who finished their studies, passed their final examinations, and were awarded their college degrees in a brief private ceremony in July 1775. Bushnell left New Haven with the other graduates, but instead of volunteering for the patriot army, he returned to Old Saybrook to continue the secret construction of the submarine that he planned to use to attach his powerful infernals to the defenseless hulls of enemy warships.

CHAPTER FOUR

Bushnell's American Turtle

DAVID BUSHNELL BUILT the world's first submarine in a shed behind his house. It was an odd-looking craft: small and oval in shape, about seven feet long, six feet high, and three and a half feet wide at its middle. It was constructed in an unusual manner: Instead of being fabricated starting with a keel (a sturdy bottom beam) supporting a timber frame that was covered with planks of wood (the traditional way of building a wooden ship), Bushnell's submarine was built from two solid pieces of a large oak tree trunk that were trimmed to fit together. It was a big project, and Bushnell, who was a frail, scholarly man, was fortunate to have a strong younger brother, named Ezra, to help him. They hired trustworthy workmen to shape the outsides of the two pieces of wood with saws, chisels, and planes, to create a pair of ovals that looked exactly like giant turtle shells and which gave the sub its popular name: the *American Turtle*. Next, the insides of the two solid wooden ovals were chiseled out with tools. When the two matching hollowed-out pieces were put together, they created a cockpit that was just large enough to hold one man. The advantage of building the body of the *American Turtle* from solid wood was that it was almost watertight: Water could seep inside only along the seam between the two wooden ovals.

As the work progressed, several other trusted workmen, including woodworkers and blacksmiths, were employed by the Bushnell brothers to work on the *Turtle*'s detailed construction. They also employed a joiner (a man who did fine woodwork) to finish the edges of the two hollowed-out pieces of wood so that they would fit perfectly into each other (using a technique known as tongue-and-groove construction). After being joined together, the narrow seam between the two ovals was caulked with oakum (a material made from rags and loose hemp and jute fibers, soaked in tar or creosote) to create a watertight seal. The oakum was forced into the seam using primitive caulking guns common in ship construction at the time. A strong, wide iron band was then wrapped and nailed over the critical seam to hold the two wooden ovals together. Next, a circular hole was cut into the top of the craft, allowing workmen to get inside and install the machinery that operated the sub.

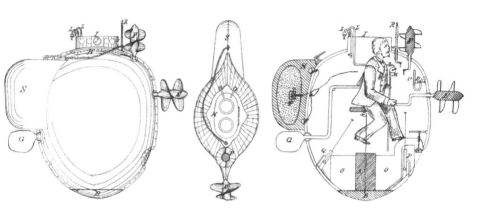

1875 ILLUSTRATION OF THE *AMERICAN TURTLE*

These pictures were drawn by U.S. Navy Lieutenant Francis M. Barber for his 1875 lecture on "submarine boats." In his presentation, Lieutenant Barber said of the *American Turtle,* "It seems, notwithstanding its failures, to have been the most perfect thing of its kind that has ever been constructed, either before or since the time of Bushnell."

The United States Navy was interested in submarines and purchased its first one in 1900 from John Holland. Named the USS *Holland,* it was powered by a gasoline engine on the water's surface and an electric motor when submerged.

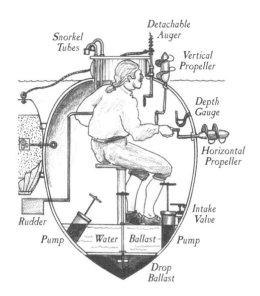

Snorkel Tubes

Detachable Auger

Vertical Propeller

Depth Gauge

Horizontal Propeller

Intake Valve

Rudder

Pump

Water

Ballast

Pump

Drop Ballast

MODERN ILLUSTRATION OF THE *TURTLE*
An artist's conception of the interior of the *American Turtle*. Note the shape of the propellers and the depiction of the pilot sitting above a ballast tank.

Let's imagine that we squeezed into the *American Turtle* through the hole that the workmen cut. We are in a cramped, windowless space that is just large enough to hold one man, whom Bushnell called the operator. He sat in the middle of a wooden beam, looking forward at an array of valves, rods, vents, cranks, screws, latches, pedals, and pumps that operated the sub. Many of these parts were made of iron by skilled blacksmiths. One iron part was a shaft on the operator's left side. In nautical terms it is called a tiller, and it was connected to a wooden rudder that Bushnell said was "hung to the hinder part [back] of the Vessel." The tiller controlled the rudder, which made the *Turtle* move left and right. There was a metal shaft in front of the operator that he could turn with a big crank held in his right hand or with a pedal at his feet. It was the same type of simple foot pedal used to turn a spinning wheel. The hand crank and foot pedal were connected by iron rods to the shaft that extended through a hole in the *Turtle*'s front (bow). At the end of the shaft, lying underwater, was an object that Bushnell called an oar. He said this oar "was formed upon the principle of the screw . . . which being turned one way, rowed the Vessel forward, and being turned the other way, rowed it backward." We believe that Bushnell was describing a propeller. One eyewitness said it was twelve inches long and five inches wide and "shaped like the arms of a windmill." Another called the oar a paddle and said that by turning it, "the machine could be propelled at the rate of about three miles an hour in still water." The *Turtle* had another propeller, facing upward, that was turned by a crank located above the operator's head.

It controlled the *Turtle*'s up-and-down motion when the vessel was underwater. In the age of sailing ships and men rowing with oars, using a propeller to move a boat was an advanced idea that has been overlooked because Bushnell referred to this mechanism as an oar.

Bushnell used water, in the manner suggested by Bourne, to make his submarine dive and resurface. By looking down from where the operator sat in the *Turtle*, we can see how it was done. Located within easy reach of the operator's feet was a round metal plunger with a spring that held it firmly in place. When he pushed down on the plunger, the spring was compressed, opening a metal disk on the outside and allowing water to flow in. When he released the plunger, the spring snapped the metal disk shut. Here are Bushnell's own words describing the process: "When the operator would descend he placed his foot upon the top of a brass valve [plunger], depressing it, by which he opened a large aperture [hole] in the bottom of the Vessel, through which the water entered at his pleasure." There was a perforated brass plate in front of the aperture to filter out any debris that might jam the delicate hand pumps used to expel the water.

We can understand the operator slowly pressing his foot on the plunger until the *Turtle* reached its desired depth; there is, however, no known account of what happened to the water when it entered the cockpit. A picture of the *Turtle* drawn in 1875 by Lieutenant Francis Barber of the U.S. Navy shows a ballast tank under the operator's bench, where he imagined the water was stored. The latest thinking is that the water simply flooded the lower portion of the cockpit and that the operator was sitting in water, perhaps up to his knees.

When he wanted to ascend, the pilot reached with his hands for the handles of the two small pumps — Bushnell called them forcing pumps — that smoothly reduced the *Turtle*'s weight by ejecting the ballast water back into the sea. An early history of submarines commented on the design: "Bushnell, a remarkable inventor, substituted a hand-pump ... for the [screw] mechanism proposed by Bourne." The two pumps aboard the *Turtle* were precision devices made out of brass by Isaac Doolittle, a New Haven craftsman described as "an ingenious Mechanic of clocks," whom Bushnell met while he attended Yale.

The *Turtle*'s cockpit was fitted with two instruments: a common pocket compass and a custom-made depth gauge. The compass told the operator the course he was steering, and a standard, easy-to-obtain pocket version was placed where it could be easily viewed. It was useful when the *Turtle* was running on the surface close to land, such as in New York harbor, but critical when the craft was underwater and the operator could hardly see his hand in front of him in the darkness.

The cockpit's depth gauge was custom-made by Bushnell based on a design described by Drebbel 150 years earlier. Bushnell described his instrument in response to an inquiry from Thomas Jefferson (a fellow inventor and scientist) as "a glass tube eighteen inches long, and one inch in diameter, standing upright, its upper end closed, and its lower end, which was open, screwed into a brass pipe, through which the external water [seawater] had a passage into the glass tube." There was a cork that rose inside the tube as the *Turtle* submerged and dropped as the sub returned to the surface.

CHAPTER FIVE

Fox Fire

SINCE BUSHNELL PLANNED to attack hostile ships at night, he needed a way to illuminate the *Turtle*'s compass and depth gauge. The obvious solution was to light a candle inside the cockpit, but an eyewitness said this idea was quickly rejected: "He has tried a candle, but that destroys the air [oxygen] so fast he cannot remain under water long enough to effect the thing [complete his mission]." The problem had Bushnell stumped until he thought of using fox fire, the greenish glow sometimes given off by rotten wood. What caused this glow was a mystery at the time, but today we know that it comes from fungi that infect decaying wood. The idea worked, and

Bushnell illuminated the critical points on the compass with bits of fox fire. North was marked with a "+," east with a "–," and particles of fox fire were glued to the tip of the compass's direction arrow. The top of the cork in the depth gauge was also coated with specks of fox fire.

However, fox fire was not the perfect solution for illuminating the *American Turtle*'s instruments because the rotting wood glowed only in warm weather. Bushnell desperately tried to find another material to light the cockpit but without success. In fact, Bushnell's Connecticut friend Dr. Benjamin Gale wrote to Congressman Silas Deane in Philadelphia asking him to contact Benjamin Franklin to "enquire of Dr. Franklin [whether] he knows of any kind of phosphorus which will give light in the dark and not consume air," adding that "he [Bushnell] now finds that the frost wholly destroys that quality in that wood." The result was that although Bushnell's submarine was a sturdy little vessel, its operation was confined to a few warm weather months by some flakes of glowing wood.

CHAPTER SIX

The Conning Tower

USING BUSHNELL'S MEASUREMENTS, a skilled blacksmith forged a round iron plate to cover the hole that had been cut into the *Turtle*'s top. The plate was attached to the wooden hull with a strong iron band and caulked around its edges. In the middle of the iron plate, the blacksmith had built a circular brass tower that is called a conning tower in a modern submarine. Bushnell's brass conning tower contained a round hatch door, just big enough for the operator to squeeze through. The hatch was hinged on one side and bolted down from the inside with screws. Bushnell described the iron plate and the brass conning tower with its hatch as "resembling a hat with its crown [brass top] and brim [iron base], which shut watertight." The hatch could also be opened from the outside in an emergency.

Other important operating equipment in Bushnell's conning tower included three holes that allowed air to enter the *Turtle* when it was cruising on the surface. They were sealed watertight with metal shutters that Bushnell said "were ground perfectly tight into their places, with emery [an abrasive material used for polishing], hung with hinges." There were also eight little round glass windows (portholes) in the tower facing in every direction, including one that looked upward. They enabled the operator to see out in all directions when he was cruising on the surface and also allowed a little daylight into the cockpit when the *Turtle* was running on the surface.

There were also two brass air pipes whose large rounded ends (Bushnell described them as "hollow spheres ... perforated full of holes") extended into the air when the *Turtle* was submerged just below the waterline. The rounded end of each of the snorkels contained three hollow wooden balls (rubber was unknown in North America at the time) under a metal plate. When the submarine dived, the pressure of the water pushed the balls upward against the metal plate

The first portrait of George Washington as commander in chief of the Continental army, painted by Charles Willson Peale. This is what Washington looked like when David Bushnell arrived in New York in the summer of 1776 with his submarine.

and closed the snorkels. They reopened when the *Turtle* returned to the surface. Here is how Bushnell described their operation: "Both air pipes were so constructed, that they shut themselves whenever the water rose near their tops, so that no water could enter through them, and opened themselves immediately after they rose above the water."

CHAPTER SEVEN

The Last Details

THERE WERE A NUMBER OF metal rods and shafts passing through the *Turtle*'s hull. The tiller rod that moved the rudder was one; the shaft that turned the bow propeller was another. The holes in the hull that these rods and shafts passed through were called joints by Bushnell, and they all had to be watertight. He explained how it was done: "Whenever the external apparatus [the propeller shaft, for example] passed through the body of the Vessel, the joints were round and formed . . . and the iron rods which passed through them were turned in a lathe to fit them; the joints were also kept full of oil to prevent rust and leaking." In other words, the shafts and rods were almost the same diameter as the holes in the hull. The small space between them was lubricated and sealed with grease, a material that at the time was made from animal fat.

The dangerous effects of water pressure, called hydrostatic pressure, on an object were known in the eighteenth century, and Bushnell took them into account when he designed his submarine by making all of its seals and joints strong and watertight. He also used the wooden bench in the cockpit to strengthen the *Turtle* against the underwater pressure pushing against its body. Using the scientific language of the day, Bushnell described the beam's special function: "The body of the Vessel was made exceedingly strong: and to strengthen it as much as possible, a firm piece of wood was framed, parallel to the conjugate diameter [at a right angle to the *Turtle*'s walls], to prevent the sides from yielding to the great pressure of the incumbent [resting] water in a deep immersion. This piece of wood was also a seat for the operator." In another reference to water pressure damaging his vessel when it was submerged, Bushnell said that the iron plate covering the opening in the top of the *Turtle* "was made, in such a manner, as to give its utmost support to the body of the Vessel against the pressure of the water."

Fortunately, the *Turtle* was designed to submerge to a maximum depth of only twenty feet. If it had gone any deeper, the operator would have encountered serious problems with water pressure pushing against the hull, joints, and iron bands of his craft. Since the pilot was breathing the air inside the *Turtle*, there was little pressure on his body as the submarine dived and resurfaced.

The final step was to cover the *Turtle*'s hull with tar to make it even more watertight. When the tar dried, David Bushnell had a practical, working submarine that could steer, dive, ascend, navigate, and remain submerged for up to thirty minutes. But he had to add one of his underwater mines to make it a warship and devise a way to transport, attach, and detonate it from inside the *Turtle* without killing the operator or damaging his valuable craft. "Considering Bushnell's machine as the first of its kind," said one historian, "ranks him as a mechanical genius of the first order."

Bushnell's design for transporting and exploding his mine was truly amazing. He built an egg-shaped mine made from two pieces of solid oak that were hollowed out to hold 150 pounds of gunpowder, the amount he estimated was necessary to blow a large hole in the wooden hull of a ship. This watertight wooden device was held to the stern (rear) of the *Turtle* with two metal rods that passed through matching holes in the back of the cockpit. Using a common nut-and-bolt arrangement, the mine could be detached from the *Turtle*'s back by unscrewing the nuts, which had grab handles welded on their sides.

Bushnell still had to devise a way to secure the mine to the bottom of a ship. His interesting solution was as follows: He fitted a heavy auger (drill) sticking straight up from the top of the sub that he called a "woodscrew." Its sharp, oversized metal bit protruded through a protective metal tube from the top of the sub. One report described it as "a pointed rod at top designed to be stuck into the ship's bottom." The thick auger was connected via a waterproof hole through the hull to a handle inside the cockpit. A strong piece of rope connected the tip of the auger to the mine. The idea was to bore the auger tip into the bottom of a ship from inside the cockpit, then disconnect it by unscrewing the handle. This left the mine attached to the drill bit, which was now stuck into the bottom of the ship.

There was still one step left: to activate the timing mechanism inside the mine. There are references indicating that the timing device used in the *Turtle* was built by Phineas Pratt, a Connecticut silversmith and clockmaker. His clockwork followed Bushnell's earlier design, but was modified to start ticking when the operator pulled on a rope connected to it from inside the cockpit. The detonation time was set for twenty minutes, when the metal pin attached to the main wheel of the clock would snap a gun lock and explode the gunpowder.

In an 1899 published account of the *Turtle*, the author, who identified himself only as "a careful follower of the *Turtle*," said that Bushnell's finished submarine looked like two turtle shells and its brass conning tower looked like a head peering out from its body. The resemblance to an eerie-looking creature was heightened by the glass portholes in the tower that peered out like eyes, the two snorkels that stood out like antennae, and the egg-shaped object strapped to its back. The "careful follower" claimed that when someone asked Bushnell, "Does the *Turtle* snap?" he replied, "Never, until the word is given."

CHAPTER EIGHT

Secretly Testing the American Turtle

AFTER COMPLETION, the *Turtle* was quietly moved on a wagon from the isolated shed to the nearby Connecticut River, where it was launched into the water. The event can be imagined as David and Ezra, accompanied by a few trusted workmen, drove the wagon into shallow water and lowered the *American Turtle* into the river with ropes and pulleys. They found that it floated perfectly, with its brass tower bobbing above the surface. Ezra Bushnell had already agreed to operate the sub on its combat missions. The decision allowed David to take his brother's weight, plus the weight of the *Turtle* and its mine, and add just enough lead weights (ballast) to the floor of the cockpit to get the *Turtle* to float with its conning tower sticking out of the water exactly seven inches. This was done to make the *Turtle* as small as possible when it was cruising on the surface but still allow Ezra to let in fresh air and look out the portholes. Commenting on this point, Bushnell said, "The Vessel with all its appendages [attachments], and the operator, was of sufficient weight to settle it very low in the water."

The *Turtle*, with its mine, operator, and lead ballast aboard, weighed about four thousand pounds. However, certain items could be removed — the mine and lead ballast, for example — to make it lighter for transporting it on a wagon. Some historians believe that Bushnell built a special cart to carry his submarine. However, towing the *Turtle* in the water was the easiest way to move it from place to place.

Following some preliminary adjustments and testing, the *Turtle* was towed by a sloop (a small ship with a single mast) to Poverty Island (no longer existing), a low marshy piece of land lying near the mouth of the Connecticut River, for advanced testing. According to the "careful follower," David and Ezra purchased this small island, which was infrequently used by fishermen. The Bushnell brothers wanted to use the island as their base for secret deep-water test dives of the *Turtle*. There were British spies and sympathizers everywhere, and in an effort to keep the *Turtle* a secret, the Bushnells told everyone that they were on the island to fish. They hid their submarine in an old seine house, a place where fishing nets were stored. Most of the small island was covered with tall salt grass that concealed their activities.

David invited only one person, Dr. Benjamin Gale, who was a local doctor, amateur scientist, and influential Connecticut patriot, to see his invention. Gale was impressed, and with Bushnell's permission, he wrote his friend Benjamin Franklin in Philadelphia about the "underwater machine." In a letter to Franklin dated August 7, 1775, Gale was enthusiastic in his praise of Bushnell's *Turtle*: "Give me Leave to Say, it is all Constructed with Great Simplicity, and upon Principles of Natural Philosophy, and I Conceive is not Equaled by any thing I ever heard of or Saw, Except Dr. Franklins Electrical Experiments."

Franklin visited Bushnell a few months later when he passed through Connecticut en route to a meeting at General Washington's headquarters in Cambridge, Massachusetts. According to one account, Franklin was rowed out to Poverty Island and taken to the door of the seine house. The seine-house doors were swung open, and the great Dr. Franklin laid his eyes on Bushnell's strange machine for the first time: "curious, oaken, iron-bound, many-paddled, brass-headed, window-lighted thing. It was the big fish David said he was after!"

The story of Franklin's visit makes wonderful reading, but some historians doubt that it took place. They point out that there is no known letter or official report confirming the story. Trying to decide if Franklin saw Bushnell's submarine is work for a history detective.

Let's look at the facts. We know that Franklin was a curious man and a great scientist who would have enjoyed seeing an important new invention, especially one that would help the American patriots in their fight against Britain. As a member of the Secret Committee of the Continental Congress, Franklin also had an official interest in the *Turtle*: His committee's job was to help supply Washington's army with military equipment. We can account for the absence of a report about the *Turtle* because Franklin's committee worked behind closed doors and kept few records, which they later destroyed.

A study of Franklin's whereabouts in 1775 puts him in Connecticut at the same time that Bushnell was testing his submarine. He is known to have left Philadelphia on October 6, 1775, to attend a meeting in Cambridge with General Washington and arrived in Cambridge on the night of October 15. It was dangerous for Franklin to make the trip by ship because the Royal Navy was patrolling the coastal waters and would have loved to capture a "high rebel" at sea. Traveling overland, Franklin had to cross Connecticut, and the best road through the colony, called the Boston Post Road, followed the coastline with good inns and taverns to attract travelers. The Boston Post Road crossed the Connecticut River via a ferry that was located less than one mile from Poverty Island.

There is more! We know that Franklin visited his friend Dr. Gale when he traveled across Connecticut in October 1775. In an obvious reference to the *Turtle*, Gale wrote a friend a month later, "The trials I mentioned to have been made since Dr. Franklin's being here, was the explosion [testing the mine], which prov'd beyond expectation." Also, someone (Franklin?) was talking about Bushnell's invention in Cambridge, because an army officer wrote Congressman John Adams in late October 1775, "The famous Water Machine from Connecticut is every Day expected in Camp. . . . I wish it might succeed and the

Ships be blown up beyond the Attraction of the Earth for it is the only Way or Chance they [the British] have of reaching St. Peters Gate." The evidence points to Franklin seeing the *Turtle* and talking about it when he arrived at army headquarters.

CHAPTER NINE

Bushnell Appeals for Help

BUILDING THE *AMERICAN TURTLE* was an expensive undertaking, and Bushnell was using his own money to build and test it in an effort to keep its existence a secret. But at the urging of his friend Dr. Gale, Bushnell contacted Connecticut's patriotic Council of Safety for help. They were interested and sent Lieutenant Governor Matthew Griswold to inspect the *Turtle*, which was under construction at the time. Griswold gave a favorable report, but the colony had more urgent demands, including providing food, weapons, clothing, and gunpowder for its troops, and the council was able to offer Bushnell only a small sum to continue his work. Insulted by their trifling offer,

The Colony of Connecticut, Including the Route of the *American Turtle* to New York City

———— ◉ ————

THE CLOSE-UP VIEW of Connecticut on the following pages is from a larger map titled "A Map of the Most Inhabited Part of New England." The places associated with the story of the *American Turtle* have been labeled. They are Old Saybrook, the site of the Bushnell homestead; New Haven, where David Bushnell attended Yale College; and Poverty Island, where the *American Turtle* was secretly tested.

When completed, Bushnell's submarine was transported by a coastal sloop across Long Island Sound to New York City. The sloop's probable route is marked on the map. The ship was probably unarmed, or carrying a few small cannons, and would have sailed close to the Connecticut coast so that it could duck into a shallow inlet or small harbor if a Royal Navy cruiser approached.

NEW HAVEN
NEW YORK CITY
COLONY
KONEKT
LONG ISLAND SOUND
LONG ISLAND
NEWHAVEN COUNTY
FAIRFIELD COUNTY
THE HIGH LANDS
HEMPSTEAD PLAINS
The Land inclosed between the double Boundary Lines is the Oblong or 69,000 Acres granted by Konekticut to New York
Livingstone
Rhinbek
Pakepsy
Kingstown
Sheffield
Ankram
Canaan
Norfolk
Colebrook
Granville
Westfield
Sharon
Goshen
Cornwall
Dover
Litchfield
Kent
Harwinton
Farmington
Torrington
New Hartford
Winchester
Simsbury
Waterbury
Woodbury
New Fairfield
Kensington
Southington
Wallingford
Durham
New Millford
Newtown
Danbury
Derby
Reading
Ripton
Guilford
Stratford
Ridgfield
New Haven
Brentford
Milford
Bedford
Fairfield
Norwalk
Stamford
Greenwich
Rye
Chester
Courtland
Haverstraw
Huntingdon
Oyster Bay
Hempstead
Jamaica
Flushing
Flatbush
Brookland
Flatland
Southhold
Robins Isle
Diana
Sharp Point
Cranes Point
Eatons Neck
Horse Neck
Hog Neck
Setalket
Wading
Bergben

and trying to keep his project a secret, he refused the money and continued construction on his own. He kept the handful of craftsmen working with him on the job by appealing to their patriotism and assuring them that he would get a big reward when his submarine succeeded and he would share the money with them.

Bushnell made a more vigorous attempt, in February 1776, to get outside funding for his submarine. This time he made a personal appearance before Connecticut's governor, Jonathan Trumbull, and the Council of Safety with a request for money for his "machine contrived to blow [up] ships." The council was impressed with his progress, declaring his machine "to be a work of great ingenuity" and voted him the sum of sixty pounds, Connecticut currency (a large sum of money at the time), to continue his experiments "with expectations of proper public notice and reward" if he was successful. Bushnell now had financial backing and official support, including the patronage of "Brother Jonathan," Governor Jonathan Trumbull, whose circle of friends included George Washington, the commander in chief of the Continental army.

CHAPTER TEN

The Turtle Goes to War

ARMED WITH the money provided him by Connecticut, Bushnell was able to complete his testing. In the meantime, the focus of the war had moved from Boston to New York City, and hundreds of enemy warships and transports were anchored in New York harbor in preparation for an attack on the rebel-held city.

Bushnell's new patron, Governor Trumbull, arranged for the *Turtle* to be transported to General Washington in New York. The secret shipboard arrival of Bushnell's masterpiece in New York, in early July 1776, created a sensation among the few senior officers who were told about its existence. One of them was General Israel Putnam of Connecticut, who was in command of all the

American troops defending the city. Putnam had a lot of responsibility, and he had two young assistants (aides-de-camp), David Humphreys and Aaron Burr, to help him. We believe that Putnam, too busy to go himself, sent his aides to examine the *Turtle* and report back. Humphreys described it as a "wonderful machine . . . altogether different from anything hitherto devised by the art of man." In one of the few known references to Bushnell's appearance, Humphreys said the inventor was too feeble to permit him to perform the labor of rowing the *Turtle*. Based on glowing reports, Putnam became another *American Turtle* fan. Fortunately, the British did not share his confidence in the rebels' secret weapon.

We are just becoming aware of the intensity with which the British and Americans were spying on one another during the Revolutionary War. In addition to spies, informers, and sympathizers, the British had Dr. Benjamin Church on their payroll. He was an important member of the Massachusetts Provincial Congress and kept the British informed of American plans until his mistress was caught trying to pass one of his coded reports to a British agent. The Americans were no laggards in the spying game, and their early accomplishments included stealing important papers from British headquarters. When the rebels began printing paper money, the British joined in and started printing and circulating counterfeit American bills to undermine the people's confidence in the currency. Both sides were also active throughout the war ambushing army couriers, reading each other's mail, interrogating prisoners and deserters, and recruiting code breakers to decipher captured coded messages. General Washington, in particular, has emerged as a spymaster operating a large ring of agents and informers. He disguised this important aspect of his work by claiming that he had no knowledge of intelligence operations. In this heated scene of spying, it was difficult to keep the *Turtle*'s existence a secret. In fact, the British knew about the *Turtle* while it was being built in the shed at the Bushnell homestead.

The source of British information was the tavern keeper in the town of Killingworth, where Dr. Gale lived. The tavern keeper also served as the town's postmaster and, unknown to anyone in the community, he was a loyalist (a colonist who sided with Britain during the Revolutionary War). He belonged to a spy network run by William Tryon, the royal governor of New York. The tavern keeper (name unknown) was secretly opening and reading Dr. Gale's correspondence and passing any useful information on to Tryon, including news about a rebel "underwater machine." On November 16, 1775, for example, Tryon informed Vice Admiral Shuldham in Boston, "The great news of the day with us is now to Destroy the [Royal] Navy, a certain Mr. Bushnell has compleated his Machine." The postmaster continued to read Gale's mail, with additional information about the *Turtle* being passed on to British headquarters. However, it seems that the Royal Navy did not take the threat of a rebel submarine seriously, or was too busy with other, more pressing matters to send a warship to Poverty Island to investigate.

The Americans, however, including George Washington, were interested in Bushnell and encouraged his work. Writing after the war, Washington mentioned his support of the inventor: "Bushnell is a man of great Mechanical powers — fertile of invention — and a master in execution — He came to me in 1776 recommended by Governor Trumbull and other respectable characters who were proselites [converts] to his plan. . . . That he had a machine which was so contrived as to carry a man underwater at any depth he chose, and for a considerable time & distance, with an apparatus charged with Powder which he could fasten to a ships bottom or side & give fire to in any given time . . . are facts which I believe admit of little doubt."

Soon after arriving in New York, the project suffered a serious blow when Ezra Bushnell became ill. He probably contracted camp fever, the vague medical term used at the time to describe the variety of diseases that had plagued armies for centuries. Ezra had been working with his brother for the last year building and testing the *Turtle*. Finding another person to operate the sub would not be an easy task as it required someone of courage, skill, and great physical strength. General Samuel Holden Parsons came to Bushnell's rescue by recruiting three volunteers, from the Connecticut regiments under his command, who were willing to go on a dangerous mission. After working with all three, Bushnell selected Ezra Lee, a twenty-seven-year-old army sergeant and sailor by profession, from Lyme, Connecticut. Having made his choice, Bushnell and Lee went into a crash program preparing for the *Turtle*'s first combat mission. Writing years later about his training, Ezra Lee said that they transported the *Turtle* to Long Island Sound, "and on our way practised with it in many harbours." By early September, Bushnell felt that Sergeant Lee was ready to sink an enemy ship.

CHAPTER ELEVEN

A Desperate Situation

ON THE NIGHT OF the *Turtle*'s attack, the two American whaleboats towing the sub got as close as they dared to the enemy fleet before they cast off the towropes and quietly rowed back to the safety of New York City. As soon as the towlines were cast off, Sergeant Lee, who was inside the *Turtle*, swung into action and began turning the propeller that moved the tiny vessel forward. He was cruising along with the sub's dull brass tower sticking out seven inches above the surface — just high enough to get a good look through the tiny glass portholes at the hundreds of enemy warships and transports in the harbor. The hatch door was closed, but fresh air was coming in through the three air vents in the tower and the two snorkels. In the darkness, through his little portholes, Lee could see the outline of a big British warship looming ahead of him. It was his target, the mighty HMS (His Majesty's Ship) *Eagle*, the flagship of the British fleet and the symbol of King George III's naval power in America.

The attack by Bushnell's *Turtle* was a desperate measure by the rebels to help prevent New York City from falling into enemy hands. The British were closing in on the city. General Washington's army undertook a defense plan for New York that included fortifying western Long Island (Brooklyn). The British attacked there first and badly defeated Washington's forces at the Battle of Long Island (August 27, 1776). Somehow, the remaining American soldiers managed to retreat back to Manhattan Island following their terrible defeat. From their fortifications on Manhattan, the rebels watched the British moving barges and men up the East River in preparation for an attack. The British were also probing the American defenses on the western side of the island, which faced the Hudson River (or North River, as it was also called at the time).

The urgency of the *Turtle*'s mission is highlighted in a confidential message from the American general Parsons to a fellow officer dated September 5, 1776 (just two days prior to the *Turtle*'s attack on the *Eagle*). Identifying the *Turtle* as "the Machine designed to attempt blowing Up the Enemy's Ships," Parsons requested a small craft to transport it to the New York docks, "as all Things are now ready to make the Experiment [attack], I wish it may not be delayed, tho' the Event is uncertain the Experiment under our present Circumstances is certainly worth trying."

From the beginning of the campaign, sea power was the key to who would possess New York City, and the Americans — with virtually no navy — were at a serious disadvantage. General Charles Lee (no relation to Sergeant Ezra Lee), an experienced former British officer who had joined the rebels, warned General Washington months earlier not to attempt to hold New York: "What to do with the city, I own puzzles me, it is so encircled with deep, navigable water, that whoever commands the Sea must command the town." He advised Washington to burn the city and retreat into the interior. But Washington was determined to defend the place, especially since the Continental Congress insisted that the city should be defended. The British were equally determined to seize New York because of its strategic location and excellent harbor. Since the British were obliged to transport all of their war materials and most of their food and troops from Britain, the excellent port facilities at New York were vital to the British war effort.

The king dispatched an armada of warships, the largest fleet ever sent overseas from Britain up to that time, to support the 35,000-man army his government had assembled to seize New York. One observer told how "onlookers gazed with awe on a pageant such as America had never seen before — five hundred dark hulls, forests of masts, a network of spars and ropes, and a gay display of flying pennants." The fleet, which was anchored in New York harbor just out of range of American artillery, included a number of big three-deck goliaths called men-of-war, one of which was the *Eagle*. Mounting sixty-four big cannons, monster ships like the *Eagle* were the most sophisticated war machines of their day and represented the most advanced technology of the late eighteenth century. The British government also sent an experienced naval officer to command its fleet: Admiral Lord Richard Howe, known affectionately to his men as Black Dick because he was a solemn, deep thinker. Although a serious man of few words, he was always ready for action. In one story, a sailor said, "I think we shall fight today. Black Dick has been smiling."

David Bushnell was another deep thinker, whose engineering marvel was moving silently toward the *Eagle* while Admiral Howe lay sleeping in his great cabin at the stern of his flagship. He had anchored several of his warships, including the *Eagle*, near Bedloe's Island (now Liberty Island — the island on which the Statue of Liberty stands), which lies about two miles from colonial New York's waterfront. The *Eagle* had been anchored there for several days, so the Americans knew its exact position. It could also be identified by the admiral's flag that was flying from its masthead. An eyewitness described the scene: "In the bay below N. York the british fleet made a great display; the no. [number] of the vessells of all sizes amounted to about 300 [there were actually more than 400 British ships in the harbor]; and as they spread their sails to dry — after a rain — they covered a large extent of the water. The admirals ship — the Eagle of 64 guns appeared in full sight, known by its flag."

CHAPTER TWELVE

The Vigilant Enemy

BESIDES THE FATIGUING AND COMPLICATED operation of the *Turtle*, Sergeant Lee also had to worry about being spotted by the enemy as he approached the *Eagle*. He had to cruise on the surface as long as possible since it was impossible to see anything once he submerged into the murky water, and he wanted to get close to the ship before descending into the darkness. The problem with this tactic was that the British were alert and watching for attempts by the rebels to capture or sink their ships. While they had heard rumors from spies that the Americans had a submarine, they were watching for rebel boarding parties and fireships. The use of boarding parties was an age-old technique in which

Ship of the line

Frigate

Warships of the Eighteenth Century

———— ◎ ————

THIS ILLUSTRATION SHOWS the larger types of warships used in the American Revolution and their relative size. The chart is only a general guide, as there were numerous variations and modifications from these basic designs.

The largest warships at the time were known by several different names: ships of the line, capital ships, and men-of-war. They were the eighteenth-century equivalent of modern battleships. Ships of the line had three masts and carried a minimum of sixty-four guns, mounted on three decks. Because of their large size, they were hard to maneuver and were brought into action when enormous firepower was needed, such as an attack on an enemy fleet. The *American Turtle*'s first target was a ship of the line: the HMS *Eagle*.

Sloops of War

Bombs

Fire Ships

The next warship in size, called a frigate, was in many ways the most feared ship of the period. Frigates were fast, with plenty of firepower, and tended to operate alone. Many of the Royal Navy frigates used in the Revolutionary War mounted thirty-two cannons carried on one deck. A frigate could attack smaller seaports or swoop down on rebel merchant ships.

Every young officer in the Royal Navy dreamed of commanding a frigate. Not only was there action, but there was also the chance to get rich by capturing enemy ships (prizes), which were sold, with a handsome share of the proceeds (prize money) going to the frigate's captain.

The *American Turtle*'s second and third failed attacks were against three Royal Navy frigates (the *Phoenix*, the *Roebuck*, and the *Tartar*) that were anchored in the lower Hudson River, just below the rebels' Fort Washington–Fort Lee defense line.

armed men in boats tried to sneak up and climb aboard a ship, especially at night, and capture it by overwhelming its crew.

A fireship (or a flotilla of fireships) was another ancient feature of naval warfare. In this technique, the deck and rigging of a surplus ship were covered with fast-burning tar and other combustibles. Sometimes kegs of gunpowder were placed deep in the hold. The attackers would attempt to slip the fireship, manned by a few volunteers, among enemy vessels at night and aim it at a prime target. The courageous crew would set their fireship ablaze before escaping in boats. If successful, the burning hulk would ram the enemy ship and engulf it in flames. If there was gunpowder aboard the fireship, it would be ignited by the spreading fire, throwing a shower of burning wood onto the decks and rigging of enemy ships, adding to the destruction. An uncontrolled fire aboard a wooden warship with a powder magazine (the place deep in the hold where gunpowder was stored) was the fastest way to blow it up or severely damage it.

In wartime, ships at anchor observed the direction of the wind and currents and knew from which direction a fireship had to come and positioned their anchored ships to present the smallest possible target. The moored ships also had men equipped with axes who could cut the anchor cable if a flaming wreck got too close. The rebels had sailed fireships against three Royal Navy frigates anchored in the Hudson River just a month prior to the *Turtle*'s attack. The assault had nearly succeeded, and the British were watching for new fireship attacks against their valuable fleet.

Concerned about boarding parties and fireships, Admiral Howe had lookouts and sentries posted throughout the fleet, especially at night. Hundreds of men were peering out into the darkness, looking for any unusual activity in the water, while boatloads of armed sailors patrolled the surrounding waters, alert to any unfamiliar movement or sound. Apparently the rebel boats towing the *Turtle* were spotted, as evidenced by the log of the HMS *Asia* for the night of September 7–8, 1776 (the night the *Turtle* made its attack). The *Asia* was anchored in the harbor near the *Eagle* and reported, "Sent 4 Boats to the Assistce [assistance] of the Advanced Guard p [per] Signal." Clearly a guard boat had seen unknown boats in the water and sounded the alarm, which caused the *Asia* to send four additional boats to investigate. The *Eagle* was anchored nearby, and its log reported the same incident, saying that it fired a gun (probably a small cannon called a swivel gun) to acknowledge the alarm: "Ships log, HMS *Eagle*, Captain Henry Duncan commanding [Admiral Lord Howe commanded the entire fleet]...At $1/2$ past 10 [P.M.] the out guard boats [the boats patrolling the farthest away from the *Eagle*] made the alarm signal, fired a gun & made the signal [perhaps a flare or whistle] for sending the guard boats to their assistance. $1/2$ past 11 fired a Gun & made the Signal to recall them." The incident was also recorded by Ambrose Serle, Admiral Howe's personal secretary, who was aboard the *Eagle* and wrote in his diary, "Saturday, 7th. Septr. A slight alarm happened to-night from the Enemy's Boats approaching too near; they were soon driven back by the Musketry in our Boats."

The quick response to the approach of unknown boats proved that the British were alert and guarding their valuable ships. However, they never expected an underwater attack, thus allowing the *Turtle* to slip in among their fleet. Nevertheless, Lee had plenty to worry about. He could still be spotted by the guard boats circling the area or the sentries stationed aboard the warships. Even the off-duty crew members aboard the fleet could quickly respond to trouble: They slept with their clothes on and were ready to leap to their feet if the alarm was sounded, when they would come rushing on deck with pikes, cutlasses, muskets, and pistols that they kept nearby. The crew was also armed with large-caliber muskets called wall guns that fired musket balls at long range. Of even more concern to Lee were the cannons aboard the warships. He knew that some of these smashers were loaded with grapeshot, a deadly cartridge designed to tear apart anything in the water at close range.

CHAPTER THIRTEEN

The Patriotism of Ezra Lee

EZRA LEE WAS SELECTED to operate the *Turtle* because he was intelligent, courageous, and strong. Strength and endurance were important because muscle power operated everything on board the *Turtle*. There were no engines, electric motors, or steam engines at the time of the American Revolution (although James Watt patented a steam engine in Britain in 1769), and wind and water power were impractical to propel the *Turtle*. Bushnell realized early on that he lacked the physical strength and endurance to operate the sub in a combat situation, so someone else had to take his place. Ezra Lee also had the conviction to carry out his dangerous mission in the name of American liberty and independence. He was in the American army at New York in July 1776 when a courier arrived in the city with the news that the Continental Congress in Philadelphia had declared that the thirteen colonies were no longer fighting for a "redress of their grievances with England" but for independence and had declared themselves a new and separate nation. As a soldier, Lee heard the Declaration of Independence being read by order of General Washington: "General Orders, Head Quarters, New York, July 9th 1776. The Honorable the Continental Congress, impelled by the dictates of duty, policy and necessity, having been pleased to dissolve the Connection which subsisted between this Country, and Great Britain, and to declare the United Colonies of North America, free and independent STATES: The several brigades are to be drawn up this evening on their respective Parades, at six Oclock, when the declaration of Congress [the Declaration of Independence], shewing [stating] the grounds & reasons of this measure, is to be read with an audible voice."

Ezra Lee stood in formation that evening with his fellow soldiers in Captain David F. Sill's company of the 10th Connecticut Regiment listening to "The Unanimous Declaration of the Thirteen United States of America," which included these stirring words: "That these United Colonies are, and of Right ought to be Free and Independent States; that they are Absolved from all Allegiance to the British Crown, and that all political connection between them and the State of Great Britain, is and ought to be totally dissolved." Two months later, Sergeant Lee was risking his life in a bid to help his infant nation breathe life into the Declaration of Independence.

CHAPTER FOURTEEN

The Turtle Attacks the Eagle

LEE GOT HIS TINY SUBMARINE as close as he dared to the giant *Eagle* on the surface. In fact, he reported that he could hear voices from the *Eagle*'s deck as he silently approached it with his conning tower just above the surface of the water and his air vents open. Then, when he decided that it was too dangerous to proceed any farther on the surface, he quickly closed the shutters of the air vents and pushed his foot on the plunger. Seawater flooded into the *Turtle*, and the craft began to dive beneath the waves. The first submarine attack in history had begun.

Inside the *Turtle*, Ezra Lee was straining to keep his tiny craft on course, with his left hand moving the tiller

The Ratzer Map

The Plan of the City of New York, in North America:
Surveyed in the Years 1766 & 1767

———— ◉ ————

THE MAP ON THE FOLLOWING PAGES IS one of the most beautiful and prized maps in American history. Only a section of the map is shown to illustrate the route of the *American Turtle* in its bid to sink the *Eagle*, anchored near Bedloe's Island in New York harbor.

The original map was drawn by Lieutenant Bernard Ratzer, a Swiss-born engineer serving in the British army. He sent his drawing to England, where it was printed and sold in stores and bookstalls. The original printer misspelled *Ratzer* as *Ratzen*, resulting in this famous map being identified by two different names.

Maps have always been a major source of information,

and people purchased the Ratzer map before the Revolutionary War to learn about New York City, which was a major commercial center in the British Empire. Once the war started, the Ratzer map became an important source for both the Americans and British to plan their military operations in and around New York. It is probable that George Washington and his generals had a copy of the Ratzer map spread out before them during the summer of 1776 to plot the position of enemy warships in New York harbor and to plan their defense of the city.

Another wartime interest in the map was by people in Britain who had family members and friends fighting in America. They wanted maps that showed the places mentioned in the letters being sent home by their relatives and friends. In addition, British newspapers carried war news from America, and the public purchased detailed maps to help them follow the events of the war.

Attach Route of the Turtle.
Sept. 6-7, 1776

WHITEHALL SLIP

BEDLOE'S ISLAND

bar while his right hand and both feet were turning the bow propeller as he watched the dimly lit compass in front of him. Despite his inventive genius, Bushnell could not eliminate problems caused by the strong tides and uncertain currents in New York harbor. To compensate for this, Bushnell relied on the *Turtle*'s compass, propeller, and rudder and Sergeant Lee's strength to hold his craft on course. Lee only had the oxygen, or "vital air," as it was called at the time, that was trapped inside the sub to breathe, and he could remain underwater for only half an hour before he had to surface again for fresh air. The trapped air inside the pitch-black cockpit soon became hot and stale, and we can picture Lee wearing only breeches and a shirt (underwear was not commonly worn in the eighteenth century), straining every muscle and nerve, and dripping with sweat, as he approached the mighty *Eagle* underwater.

CHAPTER FIFTEEN

The Crucial Moment

THE CLIMAX OF YEARS of hard work was about to take place as the daring Sergeant Lee dived the *Turtle* under the hull of the *Eagle*. Groping around in the dark, he felt the sub bang against the wooden hull of the big warship. Lee pushed on the metal plunger again to let in more seawater, and the *Turtle* bounced and scraped its way down along the *Eagle*'s hull to its bottom. Certain he was under the *Eagle*'s keel, Lee moved a sweating hand up and gently cranked the top propeller clockwise until he felt the tip of the auger touch the keel of the big ship. Then he grabbed the auger crank in the darkness. The great moment had arrived. Everything had been checked and rechecked many times. Lee had to remain

calm and alert in the absolute darkness, in what could easily become his underwater coffin, as he began to twist the auger into the *Eagle*'s keel. Slowly the bit began to turn. With Bushnell, Sergeant Lee had practiced over and over again the sequence of attaching the mine to the keel: Once the bit was secure, he had to carefully untwist the auger handle, gently turn around in the cockpit and unscrew the two bolts that disconnected the mine, gingerly pull the rope that started the clock, and then run for his life. The clock had been set for twenty minutes, hopefully enough time for Lee to get far enough away before the gun lock ignited the 150 pounds of gunpowder under the *Eagle*'s keel. Bushnell had never used this much explosive underwater before, and he could only warn Lee that it was going to create a tremendous blast, enough to blow a large hole in the hull of the mighty *Eagle* and send it to the bottom of New York harbor.

Lee kept turning the auger into the *Eagle*'s keel. By now he was sweating hard in the stale hot air inside the *Turtle*'s tiny, dark compartment. Above him, the sailors aboard the *Eagle* were enjoying a balmy night, unaware of the drama that was taking place in the silent waters beneath them. Lee turned the auger as hard as he could, but it would not grab. Working fiercely in the

LEFT: The *American Turtle* attaches a mine to the hull of a ship.

short amount of time remaining, he renewed his efforts and tried with all his might to stick the drill bit into the wooden keel, but it would not take. With success so close, Lee held his course with the tiller and cautiously began cranking the *Turtle*'s bow propeller to move to another spot on the keel. Suddenly, Lee lost control, and the tiny submarine was caught by the tricky tide and tossed to the surface with a splash.

Recalling what happened years later, Lee said, "I ... immediately rode with great velocity, and came above the surface." The intrepid Sergeant Lee said he "then sunk again like a porpoise, I hove partly about to try again," hoping that he had not been seen by the sentries aboard the *Eagle* or the guard boats circling

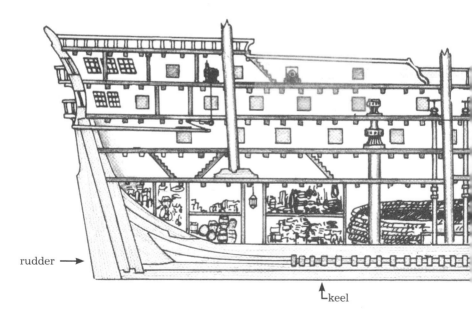

rudder →

Lkeel

the big ship. However, Lee realized that it was almost daylight, and he was exhausted from his nighttime labors. Recalling the moment, Lee said that he "gave out, knowing, that as soon as it was light the ships boats [longboats and barges] would be rowing in all directions, and I thought the best generalship was to retreat as fast as I could as I had 4 miles to go [an exaggeration of the distance], before passing Governor's Island" (an island in New York harbor, about a mile from the city, recently captured by the British), where he could be met and towed the rest of the way by friendly whaleboats.

CUTAWAY VIEW OF A WARSHIP SHOWING ITS KEEL AND RUDDER
Sergeant Ezra Lee tried to attach the *American Turtle*'s mine to the keel of the *Eagle*, forward of the rudder.

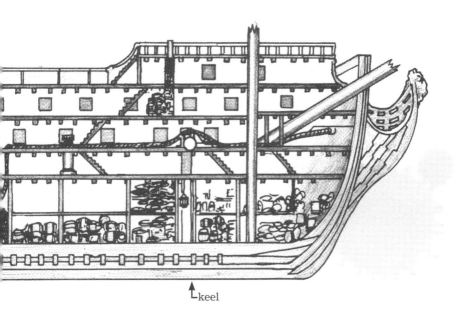

ᴸkeel

Lee began moving back across the harbor as the sun was rising, and he tried to stay underwater as much as possible to keep from being seen. However, he had to surface periodically to take in fresh air and check his bearings. As he approached Governor's Island, he surfaced to check his location. The "careful follower" said that the British soldiers on the island spotted the strange craft in the water, "such a curious boat as it is, with turret of brass bobbling up and down, sinking, disappearing — coming to the surface again in a manner wholly unaccountable." As Lee peered through his tiny glass portholes, he saw a barge pull away from Governor's Island with armed men aboard. Realizing that it was rowing hard to investigate the strange little craft, Lee began pedaling and cranking with all his remaining strength.

In a desperate bid to increase his speed, he decided to release the heavy mine to reduce the *Turtle*'s weight. Trying to remain calm, Lee turned around in the cockpit and rapidly unscrewed the nuts that held the mine. Then he turned back around and untwisted the handle of the auger that caused the watertight mine to separate from the *Turtle*. It splashed to the surface, where it was spotted by the men in the pursuit boat. Unnerved by this new and strange-looking object floating in the water, they decided to call off their chase and row back to safety.

Lee was being towed into Whitehall dock twenty minutes later when an explosion rocked the harbor. The mine had worked perfectly. Watching the blast from the dockside, the rough-edged General Putnam was heard yelling out jubilantly, "God's curse 'em, that'll do it for 'em." From the decks of their warships, the British heard the loud explosion and watched a huge column of water soar into the sky to an incredible height. According to one account, it was "speculated that the display . . . was produced by a bomb, a meteor, a water-spout or an earthquake."

Gunpowder in the
American Revolution

—————— ◉ ——————

GUNPOWDER WAS A PRECIOUS commodity
for the Americans during the Revolutionary War, and
the 150 pounds of explosives required by the *Turtle*'s
mine represented a substantial outlay by the rebels. For
example, a typical cannon at the time required 4 pounds
of powder to be fired. Therefore, a cannon could be fired
about 35 times with 150 pounds of powder.

Gunpowder was so valuable that it was commonly
shipped in small kegs, usually weighing twenty pounds
each, in case a keg broke or cracked while being
transported. The British prohibited the manufacturing
of powder in America, and it was in short supply at
the start of the Revolutionary War. The rebels initially
purchased all of their gunpowder from Europe and
from French- and Dutch-held islands in the Caribbean,
running it into American ports on fast ships through

the Royal Navy blockade. By 1776, when the *Turtle* was in operation, the Americans had also started their own limited production.

The large amount of gunpowder needed by the *Turtle*'s mine helps explain why it saw limited use: The Americans desperately needed their gunpowder to fire their cannons and muskets.

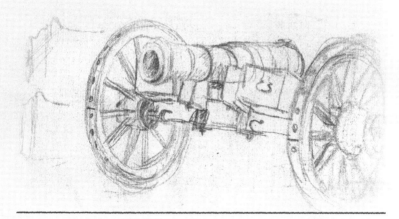

A REVOLUTIONARY WAR CANNON

Photography did not exist at the time of the American Revolution, nor were there combat artists or newspaper reporters covering the war. However, there were a few men with professional art training involved in the conflict, including the American artist-soldier Charles Willson Peale, who sketched this picture in his wartime diary.

CHAPTER SIXTEEN

The Myth of Copper-Bottomed Navy Ships

HISTORIANS HAVE SPECULATED about why Sergeant Lee was unable to drill into the bottom of the *Eagle*. The popular explanation is that, unknown to Bushnell at the time, the Royal Navy had begun to cover the bottom of their ships with copper to make them more seaworthy, and Lee was unable to make the drill bit penetrate the metal-clad hull. For example, one diarist on the scene, who called the *Turtle* a "submarine engine," alleged that Sergeant Lee "judged it as probable that the point was prevented from entering the ship by the copper sheathing." This is an interesting theory but not true. The facts are that copper-bottomed ships were already in use at the time, and Bushnell knew about them. Even if Lee had encountered a copper-clad hull, the metal was thin and soft, and the *Turtle*'s sharp auger bit would have bored right through it like a hot knife through butter. In addition, a check of Royal Navy records shows that the HMS *Eagle* was not copper-bottomed until 1782.

In any event, Lee was trying to attach the mine to the uncovered keel of the *Eagle* and not its hull. The American general William Heth mentioned this fact in his memoirs: "This machine was worked under water. It conveyed a magazine of powder, which was to be fixed under the keel of a ship." Attacking the *Eagle*'s keel made sense as it was the backbone of the ship; breaking it was the fastest way to send the big warship to the bottom.

There are logical explanations for what actually happened under the *Eagle*'s keel. One was expressed by Sergeant Lee, who said that he "was of opinion that the projecting point [drill bit] struck the head of a bolt." An interesting idea, but what probably happened was that the auger hit the thick iron plate that extended along the aft (rear) portion of the keel to hold the *Eagle*'s big rudder in place. Bushnell believed this, writing afterward that Lee had "struck the iron bar which passes from the rudder hinge. Had he moved a few inches . . . I have no

The Copper-Bottoming
of Royal Navy Ships

---◎---

THE COPPER SHEATHING of the hulls of Royal
Navy warships has been described as a bad excuse to
explain why the *Turtle* failed in its attack on the *Eagle*.

Sailors had been experimenting for a hundred years
prior to the American Revolution, looking for an effective
means to protect the hulls of ships against marine growth
(barnacles) and the ravages of a wood-eating worm called
Teredo navalis. The practical, but expensive, solution

was to clad the hulls with copper. While copper-bottomed ships were not common in 1776, when the *Turtle* attacked the *Eagle*, the technique was known, and Bushnell was aware of its use.

More compelling to the story of the *American Turtle*'s attack on the *Eagle* is the fact that the copper sheathing used to protect the hull of a ship was thin and could be easily penetrated by the sharp metal drill aboard the *Turtle*. In a later attempt against Royal Navy frigates anchored in the Hudson River, Lee said that he tried to "attach the *Turtle*'s mine in the easy to reach stern projection of enemy warships." Called the counter, this stern section of an eighteenth-century ship was above water and included the captain's cabin.

doubt, but he would have found wood, where he might have fixed the screw."

Bushnell also claimed that Sergeant Lee was inexperienced in the handling of the *Turtle* and had been sent on the mission without adequate training after Ezra Bushnell got sick. Whatever happened, the misfortune highlights a serious problem with the *Turtle*'s design: Its operator was sightless underwater and forced to grope his way blindly around his objective.

CHAPTER SEVENTEEN

Seeing Underwater

IT TOOK MORE THAN one hundred years to solve part of the problem of seeing underwater when, in 1901, the American inventor Simon Lake perfected the collapsible submarine periscope, which allowed the submarine crew to see the surface when submerged. Like Bushnell, Lake got many of his ideas by studying the work of earlier inventors, including Johannes Gutenberg, most famous as the inventor of the printing press. Gutenberg sold primitive periscopes, as early as 1470, to pilgrims at religious festivals so that they could see over the heads of the crowd in front of them. The latest submarines use non-penetrating periscopes, which employ a high-resolution digital camera on the surface that transmits an electronic image through cables to the submarine's control room.

A second big technological breakthrough in underwater navigation was needed to be able to see below the surface. Writing in 1902, on the eve of the modern submarine, one author described the problem: "You may of course throw out a torpedo or so with as much chance of hitting a ship as you would have if you were blindfolded, turned round three times and told to fire revolver shots at a charging elephant." The same author explained that, at first, inventors believed that some daylight would come down through the water to help see, "but it is now acknowledged that once below the surface the boat [submarine] is in impenetrable darkness." He proposed using a powerful "electric projector," or underwater searchlight, that could light up a path for the craft to see underwater, but this idea never worked. The problem was solved with the invention of sonar. Perfected during World War II, sonar sends a sound wave through the water. When the signal hits something in the water, it bounces back another signal (a pinging sound) that is expertly read on the submarine's sonar screen, creating an outline of the underwater object and showing its distance and depth from the sub.

CHAPTER EIGHTEEN

The Turtle in the Hudson River

HAVING COME SO CLOSE to success, Bushnell and his team made a second attempt to blow up a Royal Navy warship in early October. The military situation in New York City had changed drastically since Sergeant Lee's attempt against the *Eagle* a month earlier. The British army landed on Manhattan Island on September 14, 1776, overwhelmed the weak American forces, and occupied the city that night while Washington's army hastily retreated to the hilly northern region of Manhattan Island (today's Washington Heights). They dug in there, protected by two big American forts whose purpose was to keep Royal Navy warships from sailing up the Hudson River. The two American forts guarding the lower Hudson were Fort Washington, on upper Manhattan, and Fort Lee, almost directly across the river in New Jersey. The Americans had also rigged a string of barriers across the river between the two forts called chevaux-de-frise (sha-vṓ-de-frēz´). Like Bushnell's *Turtle*, these barriers were another American invention to counter the powerful Royal Navy. Said to be the idea of Benjamin Franklin, they were thick tree trunks with sharp metal spikes that projected upward from the river bottom. The idea was that they would rip open the hull of any ship that dared to sail past them.

Three powerful enemy frigates were anchored in the Hudson River just below the line of chevaux-de-frise: the *Phoenix*, the *Roebuck*, and the *Tartar*. They were a menacing sight to the nearby American soldiers but a tempting target for the *Turtle*. Once again, Sergeant Lee swung into action at the helm of the little submarine. After a long discussion with Bushnell, it was agreed that Lee would attach the mine to the exposed stern of one of the frigates. The *Turtle* was launched from Fort Washington and approached the enemy flotilla underwater. However, its conning tower was spotted by an alert sentry, who sounded the alarm, sending the *Turtle* scampering back to safety. Another attempt was made by a different, unknown operator to sink one of the three frigates, but it also failed, as the *Turtle* was swept away by the strong current. The operator was lucky to get the sub back to Fort Washington.

The underlying reason for the failure of Bushnell's *American Turtle* was that it was complicated to operate. Built prior to the invention of electric motors, steam turbines, and gasoline engines, everything aboard the tiny craft was human powered. To illustrate the point, historian Alex Roland described the sequence of actions that the operator had to perform, in complete darkness, to attach a mine to the keel of a ship: "Push the foot valve to admit water . . . pump out water to stabilize at the proper depth; turn the horizontal [bow] propeller . . . steer . . . and watch the compass to close on the hull of the enemy ship; estimate the distance traveled, pump more water out with his free hand and turn the vertical propeller clockwise with his other hand in order to bring the *Turtle* up into contact with the hull; use the horizontal screw (left hand) and rudder (right elbow) to stay in position while turning the auger into the bottom of the hull." It's amazing that Lee got as close as he did, given the many difficult and fatiguing tasks he had to perform while he was locked up in a tiny space.

Chevaux-de-frise

———— ◎ ————

LACKING A NAVY TO MATCH THE BRITISH, the Americans tried several ingenious devices to even the odds. Two ideas they tested were Bushnell's submarine and the barricades called chevaux-de-frise, which literally translates from French as "horses of Friesland."

In the region of the Netherlands called Friesland, little upright pieces of iron were thrown onto the roads in wartime to injure the hooves of enemy horses. The Americans expanded on this idea and built huge upright timbers to blockade their rivers. Benjamin Franklin is credited with the concept. A row of chevaux-de-frise was planted by the rebels across the Hudson

River and another across the Delaware River to deny the Royal Navy access to these strategic waterways. Rebel forts along the riverbanks defended the lines of chevaux-de-frise from attempts by the British to destroy them.

Bushnell had run out of money, and with the war going badly for the Americans, there were more pressing needs than an expensive, gunpowder-consuming submarine. Also, he was a civilian working with the army and, as such, never had a steady source of funding for his project. The American army, having suffered heavy losses in its bid to defend New York City, was in a desperate situation, and General Washington and his senior officers had more immediate concerns than helping Bushnell. Fearing that the British army would overrun their positions in northern Manhattan, the Americans had the *Turtle* hauled aboard an American sloop that was safely anchored at Yonkers, New York, upriver from the Fort Washington–Fort Lee defense line.

But on October 9, 1776, the *Phoenix*, the *Roebuck*, and the *Tartar* suddenly slipped their moorings and started upriver. The British had enticed a man who knew the location of the narrow channel that the Americans had left open between the chevaux-de-frise and offered him a huge reward to guide them through it. With the *Phoenix* leading the way, the three frigates sailed through the rebel gauntlet. Its captain said that the American informer was aboard his ship, "and led the way & steered . . . towards the Middle of the Dam [barrier] having Pistols laying on the Binnacle [the compass housing — located near a ship's steering wheel] telling the guide what would be his Fate if the ships should stop in their passage." The big guns at Fort Washington and Fort Lee opened fire as the frigates approached in the river below.

General Washington described the scene in a report to Congress: "About 8 o'clock this morning, Two Ships of 44 Guns each, supposed to be the Roebuck & Phoenix and a Frigate of 20 guns, with Three or Four Tenders [supply barges], got under way from about Blooming dale [a section of lower Manhattan Island facing the Hudson River] where they had been lying some time and stood with an easy southerly breeze towards our Chevaux de Frise, which we hoped would have intercepted their passage while our Batteries played upon them, But to our surprise and mortification, they ran thro without the least difficulty and without receiving any apparent damage from our Forts, tho they kept up a heavy Fire from both sides of the River."

The three warships got above the American defenses, where they could raid river towns, cut rebel communications and supply lines, encourage and arm the loyalists, and wreck American shipping. Their booty included an American schooner loaded with rum, sugar, and wine. They also sank the sloop with the *Turtle* on board; the intended victims had destroyed their attacker, prompting General Heth to say, "Its fate was truly a contrast to its design."

Bushnell claimed that he recovered the *Turtle*, and his exact words, written after the war, continue to fascinate everyone interested in the subject: "After I recovered the Vessel, I found it impossible, at that time to prosecute the design any farther." His statement is jolting because no evidence has been found to date to support his claim that he retrieved his submarine. If he did salvage the *Turtle*, what happened to it? It may have been destroyed to keep it from falling into enemy hands when Washington's army retreated deep into Westchester County, New York, in mid-October 1776. Or maybe Bushnell dismantled it and hid the parts in the hope that he would be able to reassemble it at some future time.

FORCING HUDSON RIVER PASSAGE BY DOMINIC SERRES
This painting shows the Royal Navy frigates *Phoenix, Roebuck,* and *Tartar,* along with a schooner and two supply tenders, fighting their way through the Americans' Fort Washington–Fort Lee defense line on the lower Hudson River on October 9, 1776. The *American Turtle,* launched near Fort Washington, tried unsuccessfully to sink these frigates when they were anchored in the Hudson downstream prior to their foray. The three frigates safely ran through the rebel defenses, including chevaux-de-frise planted across the river (just visible to the left of the ships in the painting) and sailed north, where they sank American ships, including the sloop carrying the *American Turtle.*

CHAPTER NINETEEN

Bushnell Continues to Fight

THE END OF THE *TURTLE*, in 1776, did not stop Bushnell's war effort, and the British heard from him again a year later with a bang. There was little enthusiasm left among the rebel leaders for his pricey submarine but great interest in his mines, and he devoted his genius to improving their design. What Bushnell devised was underwater mines suspended just below the surface by wooden barrel-shaped buoys. The underwater mines were detonated by metal rods protruding from their bodies. They would explode when any of the spring-loaded rods made contact with an object in the water. This breakthrough technology is the principle of the modern underwater mine. Bushnell called the combination of a mine and barrel (or keg) by its ancient name, *infernal*, and for good measure he fastened two of the devices together with a rope between them to increase their effectiveness. If the rope hit the hull of a ship, it would swing the mines hard against the ship and detonate them.

Bushnell found financial and moral support for his infernals in Bordentown, New Jersey, in the persons of Francis Hopkinson and Joseph Borden. Hopkinson was considered a "high rebel" by the British because he had signed the Declaration of Independence. He was a creative man who wrote poetry and music and designed the first American flag (Betsy Ross was a seamstress who made flags following Hopkinson's design).

From his New Jersey base, Bushnell planned his covert operation. Finding targets was no problem: The British had captured Philadelphia, and a fleet of Royal Navy warships and transports was anchored in the Delaware River in front of the city. Bushnell was ready to launch his infernals in December 1777 by sending them floating down the Delaware with the current to wreak havoc on the enemy. At Bordentown he delicately loaded his infernals (there were twenty of them) onto a whaleboat, which was quietly rowed downriver at night with a guide who knew the Delaware's tricky course and currents. When they got as close as they dared to Philadelphia, the crew gently lowered the infernals into the water and raced back to Bordentown. Sure enough, the deadly mines were swept downstream by the current and one pair was spotted by two boys in a boat. Their curiosity cost them their lives because they were blown up when they tried to pull one of the buoys into their boat. The other infernals reached Philadelphia on the morning of January 5, 1778, and destroyed a barge in the river, killing four men and wounding several others. The explosion in the river sounded the alarm that Philadelphia was under attack.

Drums beat the call to arms, and church bells echoed the signal, sending an army of stalwart British soldiers down to the waterfront with their muskets loaded and bayonets fixed to repel the enemy. Warships along the waterfront were cleared for action and their great guns rolled out. Horse-drawn artillery was wheeled into position, and the British commander (General Sir William Howe, the same officer who had conquered New York City in 1776, who was in Philadelphia with his American mistress, Mrs. Elizabeth Loring) was roused from his quarters to lead his troops into mortal combat. Escorted by his heavily armed bodyguards, Sir William arrived at the battlefront, where, through his glass (telescope), he observed the strange-looking objects floating downriver. Pandemonium on the Delaware! Rumors spread like wildfire through the city: the barrels floating in the river were filled with rebel soldiers who would burst forth, like the Greeks from the Trojan horse, to retake the metropolis. Back on the waterfront, the intrepid redcoats commenced shooting at the kegs in volleys of deadly musket fire. They managed to sink a few of them, while the rest glided harmlessly by with the current. Bushnell claimed that his infernals failed because he was unfamiliar with the river and "obliged to depend upon a Gentleman [his river guide], very imperfectly acquainted with that part of it, as I afterwards found."

CHAPTER TWENTY

The Battle of the Kegs

BUSHNELL'S INFERNALS FAILED to sink any enemy ships, but the story of the British running scared through the streets of Philadelphia and shooting at barrels in the river helped boost American morale and create what was arguably the most beloved patriotic poem of the Revolutionary War. Written by Francis Hopkinson, "British Valour Displayed or The Battle of the Kegs" was recited throughout the American army camps to the frequent cheers and laughter of the soldiers. Here is the complete poem:

Gallants, attend, and hear a friend
Trill forth harmonious ditty.
Strange things I'll tell, which late befell
In Philadelphia city.

'Twas early day, as poets say,
Just when the sun was rising.
A soldier stood on a log of wood
And saw a thing surprising.

As in amaze he stood to gaze —
The truth can't be denied, sir —
He spied a score of kegs or more
Come floating down the tide, sir.

A sailor, too, in jerkin blue
This strong appearance viewing,
First dammed his eyes, in great surprise,
Then said, "Some mischief's brewing.

"These kegs, I'm told, the rebels hold,
Packed up like pickled herring,
And they're come down t'attack the town
In this new way of ferrying."

The soldier flew, the sailor, too,
And scared almost to death, sir,
Wore out their shoes to spread the news,
And ran till out of breath, sir. . . .

Sir William, he snug as a flea,
Lay all this time a-snoring;
Nor dreamed of harm, as he lay warm
In bed with Mrs. Loring.

Now in a fright, he starts upright,
Awaked by such a clatter;
He rubs his eyes and boldly cries,
"For God's sake, what's the matter?"

At his bedside, he then espied
Sir Erskine at command, sir;
Upon one foot he had one boot,
And t'other in his hand, sir.

"Arise! arise!" Sir Erskine cries.
"The rebels — more the pity —
Without a boat are all afloat
And ranged before the city.

"The motley crew, in vessels new,
With Satan for their guide, sir,
Packed up in bags, or wooden kegs
Come driving down the tide, sir.

"Therefore prepare for bloody war;
These kegs must all be routed,
Or surely we despised shall be,
And British courage doubted."

THE BATTLE OF THE KEGS
A nineteenth-century artist's idea of the Battle of the Kegs.

The royal band now ready stand,
All ranged in dread array, sir,
With stomach stout, to see it out
And make a bloody day, sir.

The cannons roar from shore to shore
The small arms make a rattle;
Since wars began, I'm sure no man
Ere saw so strange a battle . . .

The kegs, 'tis said, though strongly made
Of rebel staves and hoops, sir,
Could not oppose their powerful foes
The conquering British troops, sir.

From morn to night, these men of might
Displayed amazing courage;
And when the sun was fairly down
Retired to sup their porridge.

An hundred men, with each a pen,
Or more, upon my word, sir,
It is most true would be too few
Their valor to record, sir.

Such feats did they perform that day
Against those wicked kegs, sir,
That years to come, if they get home
They'll make their boasts and brags, sir.

CHAPTER TWENTY-ONE

Bushnell Joins the Army

FOLLOWING THE Battle of the Kegs, Bushnell found himself bankrupt, having used all of his own money to build his submarine and mines on behalf of the American cause. He was a patriotic civilian, with no official status or reliable sources of funding. His submarine was expensive to build, requiring a team of skilled workers who had to be paid for their work. And where did Bushnell get all of his gunpowder? The army may have given him some, but this commodity was expensive and in short supply. No wonder Bushnell was broke and exhausted! But a grateful nation acknowledged his sacrifices, and General Washington helped Bushnell by appointing him as a captain in the newly formed Corps of Sappers and Miners (today's U.S. Army Corps of Engineers; a sap is a trench and a mine is a tunnel). He served as an officer until the end of the war, after which he returned to Connecticut to live with his brother Ezra.

CHAPTER TWENTY-TWO

A Secret Life

DAVID BUSHNELL WAS A QUIET and private person, and there is little known about his later life. Some historians say he went to France, where he built submarines to help the French in their war against Britain. Others say that after the war he went to Georgia, where he became a professor at the newly established University of Georgia. The known facts are that he lived on the family farm in Old Saybrook with his beloved brother Ezra, who was married at the time. Ezra died in 1787, leaving behind a wife and five young children. David helped them work the farm in the months following his brother's death. Then he left, and one of Ezra's children recalled years later that he sent for his belongings and was never seen or heard from again in Connecticut.

Bushnell moved to the frontier community of Warrentown, Georgia, where he assumed the name David Bush and taught school, practiced medicine, and bought and sold land. His medical knowledge was probably the result of his studies at Yale and his long friendship with Dr. Benjamin Gale. Bushnell became a wealthy man and died in 1826 in Warrentown, where he was buried. His true identity was revealed in his will, which named his brother Ezra's children as his heirs. Sadly, Bushnell's tombstone has been badly eroded by time, and its exact location is unknown.

The old farmhouse where David and Ezra lived still exists. It is privately owned and located in the modern town of Westbrook, which was created from a section of Old Saybrook. The part of Killingworth, Connecticut, where Dr. Gale lived is now the town of Clinton, Connecticut.

Sergeant Ezra Lee's Revolutionary War pension application (1818) revealed that he continued to serve in the army following his piloting of the *Turtle*, was appointed a junior officer, wintered with General Washington at Valley Forge (1777–1778), fought the British at the Battle of Monmouth (1778), and retired in 1782 with the rank of lieutenant. He returned to his

I _Ezra Lee Second Lieutenant_   *82*
do acknowledge the UNITED STATES of AME-
RICA to be Free, Independent and Sovereign States, and
declare that the people thereof owe no allegiance or obedience to George the Third, King of Great-Britain; and I
renounce, refuſe and abjure any allegiance or obedience to
him; and I do _Swear_   that I will, to the ut-
moſt of my power, ſupport, maintain and defend the ſaid
United States againſt the ſaid King George the Third, his
heirs and ſucceſſors, and his or their abettors, aſſiſtants and
adherents, and will ſerve the ſaid United States in the office of
Second Lieutenant   which I now hold, with
fidelity, according to the beſt of my ſkill and underſtanding.

Camp at Valley Forge   _Ezra Lee L.t_
13th of May — 1778
Sworn before — J Varnum B Gl

EZRA LEE'S OATH OF ALLEGIANCE

Ezra Lee signed this oath of allegiance to the United States at Valley
Forge on May 13, 1778. The document confirms that he was an officer
and supports his claim that he wintered at Valley Forge with General
Washington's ragged army.

The Civil War Submarine
CSS *Hunley*

◎

SOME PEOPLE BELIEVE that the world's first submarine was the CSS (Confederate States Ship) *Hunley*, used by the South in the Civil War (1861–1865). Like the *Turtle*, the *Hunley* was a human-powered submarine. However, instead of using a mine to sink an enemy ship, the *Hunley* was fitted with a ram: a long pole jutting out from its bow that was used to attach an explosive charge to the hull of a ship.

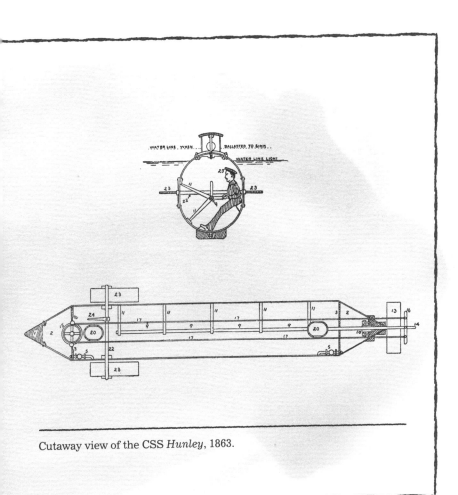

Cutaway view of the CSS *Hunley*, 1863.

homestead in Lyme, Connecticut, where he eventually became a farmer, and died in 1821. A local newspaper reported his death and mentioned his unique wartime service: "Died at Lyme on the 29th October [1821], Captain [incorrect Revolutionary War rank, although he could have been a captain in the postwar Connecticut militia] Ezra Lee, aged 72, a revolutionary officer — It is not a little remarkable that this officer is the only man, of which it can be said, that he fought the enemy upon land — upon water — and under the water."

CHAPTER TWENTY-THREE

New Discoveries

THERE ARE MANY MISSING pieces to the story of Bushnell's *American Turtle*. What happened to the *Turtle* after it was recovered from the Hudson River; did Bushnell really go to France after the Revolutionary War; and why did he move to Georgia, and assume a new identity? By remembering names like Dr. Benjamin Gale, David Humphreys, Isaac Doolittle, and Phineas Pratt; places like Poverty Island, Connecticut, and Warrentown, Georgia; and terms like *ship sinking engine* or *water machine from Connecticut*, you may see something in your future readings that means nothing to the average person but triggers your interest.

Richard DeLuca, a history buff, recently made such a

discovery. His find concerns Thomas Jefferson's interest in the *Turtle* after the Revolutionary War. Jefferson was serving as the American ambassador to France in 1784 when he made inquiries concerning Bushnell's wartime submarine. The result of his curiosity was an important letter from the inventor to Jefferson explaining how the *Turtle* was built and operated. Why Jefferson's sudden interest in the *Turtle*? The key to the answer was Mr. DeLuca's knowledge that Thomas Jefferson's secretary in France was David Humphreys, the Revolutionary War colonel who saw the *Turtle* in New York in 1776 and knew Bushnell. By reading Humphreys's unpublished letters from France, DeLuca discovered that Bushnell had started the correspondence with Jefferson: He had written Humphreys from New Haven in June 1784 (six months after the Revolutionary War ended), asking the colonel to introduce him to Jefferson in the hope of getting money from the French government to continue his experiments with "submarine navigation." The newly discovered Bushnell-Humphreys correspondence is rich in previously unknown information including Humphreys's comments that Jefferson was interested in Bushnell's "screw [propeller] to communicate motion to bodies in the air or water." Jefferson was far ahead of his time in thinking of using a propeller to move a machine through the air.

Another new source of information is Ezra Lee's recently discovered 1818 Revolutionary War pension application. It revealed that he was married with children when he volunteered for the army in 1775. Regarding the operation of the *Turtle*, Lee wrote in his application, "Ever since I went in Bushnell's Submarine Machine under the Ships in New York Bay . . . [and was] long confined partly immersed in water, taken inside to conduct it under water, I have been much troubled with Rheumatism in my legs." This statement supports the belief that the *Turtle* had no ballast tank and that seawater partially filled the cockpit when the sub was submerged. It took courage for Ezra Lee to operate the *Turtle*: He was locked in a tiny pitch-black space partially filled with seawater, twenty feet underwater, and sitting within inches of 150 pounds of volatile gunpowder. Men like Ezra Lee were ready to endure incredible hardships at the time to defend their rights and make sure that their children would live in a free and independent nation with no king or dictator to enslave them.

CHAPTER TWENTY-FOUR

Conclusion

OF ALL THE what-ifs in history, the story of the *American Turtle*'s attack on the HMS *Eagle* is one of the most fascinating. If only Ezra Lee had moved his drill bit a few inches from the *Eagle*'s iron rudder bar, he might have changed the course of history.

Despite its failure in combat, David Bushnell's submarine worked, and its creator deserves to be recognized as a proud example of American know-how along with such early American inventors as Benjamin Franklin, Eli Whitney, and Robert Fulton. He was also a dedicated patriot who devoted his inventive genius to the cause of American independence. He built the world's first submarine and equipped it for undersea warfare.

While his wartime inventions did not succeed as planned, they forced the British to divert some of their precious manpower and ships to defensive operations and spend many sleepless nights watching for Bushnell's next idea to blow them up.

Postscript

IF YOU ARE INTERESTED in reading more about Bushnell's service in the Corps of Sappers and Miners, one of the soldiers he commanded, named Joseph Plumb Martin, wrote an important eyewitness account of his experiences in the American Revolution. Martin never mentioned his commanding officer by name, but his identity is clear as he writes about his working with "the old man . . . who once sent him to the western part of Connecticut, to bring him some mathematical instruments he had left there." A modern edition of Martin's famous story is available under the title *Private Yankee Doodle*. However, the first edition of his book has a much longer title: *A Narrative of Some of the Adventures, Dangers and Sufferings of a Revolutionary Soldier, Interspersed with Anecdotes of Incidents That Occurred Within His Own Observation*. It is a plain-looking little volume with a leather spine and a yellow paper label. The book was published in Hallowell, Maine, in 1830, and it is a rare and valuable book. Look around in your attic for a copy!

Acknowledgments

I AM PLEASED TO ACKNOWLEDGE the people who helped me create this book. They are Revolutionary War historian and author John Buchanan; naval historian Captain Mike Leonard, USNR; former U.S. Navy nuclear submariner and retired president of the Electric Boat Company John K. Welch; historian David Jacobs; and Frederick Wagner, whose achievements include important research into the story of David Bushnell and his submarine.

Art Credits

Index

C

I

Infernals, 11, 13, 104–108
Inventions or Devices, 14–15

J

Jefferson, Thomas, 30, 121–122

K

King's College (Columbia University) library, 16–17

L

Lake, Simon, 93
Lee, Gen. Charles, 60
Lee, Sergeant Ezra, 57, 58–59, 63–66, 68–69, 70–72, 78, 96–97,
   123, 124
   after war, 116–117, 120
   in attack of *Eagle,* 73–78, 79–85, 88–92, 95
   inexperience of, 92
   Oath of Allegiance of, **117**
Liberty Island, 62
Long Island, Battle of, 59
Long Island fortifications, 59
Loring, Elizabeth, 106

M

Manhattan Island
   British army on, 95–96
   fortifications of, 59
   warships around, 100–103
Maps, wartime use of, 74–77
Marquess of Worcester, 13
Martin, Joseph Plumb, 126

Perrigreen Gardner Soldier
Connecticut Regiment p...
transfered to the Corps
3d Corps

West Point Jan 22d 1783.

NB – Gardners Ballance was ma...
in full for the Year 1780 altho
time in the Other Corps

Chal.s C...